FINDING SON HOUSE:
ONE SEARCHER'S STORY

A BRIEF MEMOIR

RICHARD SHADE GARDNER

Brigade Southern

Atlanta   Charleston

FINDING SON HOUSE: ONE SEARCHER'S STORY

ISBN-13: 978-1494463168

Richard Shade Gardner
Phone: 585-473-2170
Email: lakegard@frontiernet.net

Cover art and book design: Maria Friske

Printed in the USA

To Edward Keith Nobles
Catcher
Diesel Mechanic
Jazz Trombonist
and "Grandpa at the Beach"

Portions of this story have appeared in the *Rochester, NY Democrat & Chronicle, Rochester's Freezer, Q Magazine,* and *City Newspaper*; the latter earned Honorable Mention in a 2005 national survey of Arts Feature Stories.

A reading adapted from this story was presented on stage at the Downstairs Cabaret Theatre, in Rochester, as part of the presentation, *Of an Age*, produced by Gay-LeClerc Qaderi and Scotty Lyon.

Thanks to
Amy, Dan, David,
Gay-LeClerc, Jeremy, Maria, Mark,
Nicole, Scotty and Windsor.
And, of course, Son.
Okay, Evie, too.

Definitely not Canny!

PREFACE

Although today recognized globally as the father of folk blues, he lived for decades in obscurity. Alcoholism was his inseparable twin. The Word of God was a monkey on his back. He was obsessed with death. He married five times. He sent two men to the Promised Land, one by blade, one by bullet. He often didn't show up for performances; he was too drunk and he'd pawned his guitar to buy booze. When he did show up, he was content to play for the locals. Eddie J. "Son" House was the blues personified. The degree of his obscurity contrasted with the lasting and farreaching effect of his musical influence is probably unequaled by any other artist in any art form. It just so happened that the "locals" he was content to play for included two teenagers, Muddy Waters and Robert Johnson, who would carry his musical style to future generations, worldwide.

Blues radio program host, Richard Shade Gardner, was intrigued by Son House's lifelong fight with personal demons through cotton field, church pulpit, prison, juke joint, his 1930s blues recordings and finally his rediscovery, in 1964, in Rochester, New York, working for the New York Central Railroad. In 1981 Gardner caught up with the legendary octogenarian, in Detroit.

FINDING SON HOUSE: ONE SEARCHER'S STORY

FOREWORD

History has dubbed Son House "The Father of Folk Blues," based on the powerful voice and distinctive guitar style with which he delivered his rural musical messages of the trials and tribulations of the early 20th-century Southern agricultural worker. As a result of the power of his compelling live performances he was also a direct and primary influence on two significant progeny – then teenagers, in the evolution of modern music, Robert Johnson and Muddy Waters. Johnson would go on to ramp up traditional Southern acoustic blues and bring it to the doorstep of early Rock 'n' Roll. Waters would emigrate to Chicago, translate Southern Acoustic Blues into electrified Urban Blues and introduce that genre to American and European – especially British musicians, including the likes of mega-messengers such as the Beatles, the Rolling Stones, and Pink Floyd.

Imagine the evolution of rock music, outlined on an org chart. Son House might be the CEO, Waters and Johnson vice presidents of manufacturing and marketing, with Elvis, the Beatles, the Stones, and the rest of the generation that followed in sales and distribution. The board of directors, whence CEO Son received his directives, would be the generation of men and women who preceded him in the fields, before they had access to recording devices; before many had instruments; before some even had their own names. Son House was that important.

While one can chart the whereabouts and successes of Son's Pre- and Post-World War II progeny, and – in turn, their own progeny, Son, himself, was an enigma. A barely functioning alcoholic, he was missing in action, musically, more than half his life. Other than a handful of years in the 1930s and, again, in the 1960s, when he enjoyed spates of regional, then international popularity, Son was essentially silent and invisible. Few who heard his recordings, and few of the fans of his many emulators ever saw Son, knew of his whereabouts, or even if he was alive during most of his nearly nine decades.

In the 2011 book, *Preachin' the Blues; the Life and Times of Son House*, researcher and author Daniel Beaumont gives a couple paragraphs to a Son House fan who hosted a radio blues program in Rochester in the early 1980s and, at one point, decided to find out what became of Son House. Son had lived in Rochester from the 1940s to the 1970s but, following his rediscovery in 1964, and his brief performing renaissance, had dropped out of sight, perhaps died. This fan needed to know what became of the blues legend whose Grinnin' In Your Face was the sign-on and sign-off music for his weekly blues show.

I am that fan. This is the story of my search for Son House.

– RSG, Rochester, NY
   March 2015

"Son had some form of dementia by the time I met him (in the 1970s) but he still had a voice that brought the house down without any amplification. And although a lot of his guitar technique that I heard on his early recordings was gone he still made every note count with every bit of heart and soul he had. That was what I learned and try to remember at every gig I do."

Aleks Disjlenkovic, Rochester guitarist

"I first heard Son when I was fifteen or sixteen. I'd been playing guitar since I was eleven and was into the blues, at least the blues recycled through bands like Cream and the 'Stones. I was drawn to the genuine emotion of Son's music. He is the only person I've ever seen who could walk into a club, anywhere, and start playing acoustic blues and everyone – everyone – shut up and listened. Son could make his voice fill a small space or a large hall, even outside it seemed to fill it to the sky. Son could make people cry."

John Mooney, national award-winning blues musician, known for his signature Son House-influenced slide guitar work and vocal delivery.

" I first saw and heard Son House at the Gaslight Cafe, on Mac Dougal Street, in New York City, in 1965. I was nineteen. With each song he sang, he seemed to be possessed by some powerful force that took over his spirit and his playing; amazing to behold, I'd heard nothing like it before. Years later, in 1975, I officially "met" him and would hang out and play with him on the front stoop of his house or bring him to my home or to my gigs with John Mooney. He often drifted into lengthy dissertations between songs, on stage or on his front porch, about God, church, the devil and sin, and his conflict with both. My playing style today, as an upright bass player, is influenced by Son's rhythms, timing and energy. "

Brian Williams, Rochester bassist

" I've heard it said that music is what feelings sound like. There was no mistaking the depth of the feeling and the talent to express that feeling with a certainty and a rhythm to it that was so remarkable in Son House, and still is! "

Pat Magill, fan, who lives on Greig in Corn Hill and, but for a large Scotch pine tree blocking the view, she could see from her kitchen window the empty space where Son's house once sat

"I came up listening to Cream and the Stones… then there was underground FM radio which led to BB King, Bonnie Raitt, Robert Johnson and Son House. I was completely taken when I heard him, by the power and emotion. I bought his Columbia album. I knew he lived in Rochester and saw that he was playing at the Genesee Co-op on Monroe Avenue and went. He had the most powerful voice of anyone I ever heard or will hear. And I realized he was at the beginning of it all."

Mark Sampson, former Rochesterian, photographer of fine architecture and blues artists

"Then there was the moment I met Son House, a blues God as far as I was concerned. Backstage at the Village Gate (Greenwich Village, NYC) in 1965 he virtually radiated a golden light. As I watched him perform, rolling his head back, slamming the strings and almost choking on the intensity, I learned a deep lesson about the power of the music which became an inseparable part of me."

Rory Block, award-winning country blues matriarch whose album, "Blues Walkin' Like a Man," is a tribute to Son House

"It wasn't just his voice, it was his dynamics.
He was a preacher earlier in his life. He didn't have a
mike so he developed a natural vibrato from preaching.
He would go silent there on the stage, head down, then
suddenly (lifting his head) explode into My Black Mama!
– like someone dropping the needle back on the record.
He owned the audience. If I were a musician I wouldn't
want to follow him. "

*Armand Schaubroeck, co-owner of the great, great
House of Guitars and the former Black Candle,
a 1960s' coffee house in the Charlotte Neighborhood
of Rochester, where Son House was once a
main attraction*

FINDING SON HOUSE: INTRODUCTION

APRIL 1981

Mark and I squeezed out of the crowded elevator. He carried his camera, tripod and a guitar. I wielded another guitar and a backpack full of all that mysterious stuff photographers seem to need. The Otis door rolled shut behind us and our eyes began adjusting to the dimly-lit hallway. We were on the fifth floor of a Detroit project. In front of us, directly opposite the elevator, was door number 518, the one we'd driven four hundred miles, from Rochester, New York, to hopefully open. The door I'd personally been hunting down for more than a year. Many before us had looked for this door. Some found it; others had not.

BACKING UP A MOMENT

When the Beatles first visited America in February of 1964, they were met at the airport by the media hordes. Asked about their itinerary, Paul McCartney's answer included, "I'd like to visit Muddy Waters."

A reporter queried, "Where's that?"

McCartney responded, incredulously, "Don't you even know who your own famous people are?"

Rock music was still emerging at the time and the reporter, like many people, wasn't aware that British rock – in fact, rock music in general, was heavily influenced by older black American musicians.

For example, one day in 1943, McKinley Morganfield, a young agricultural worker in rural Mississippi, put away his tools, picked up his guitar and headed north for Chicago. There, he resurrected a nickname bestowed on him in childhood by his grandmother – Muddy Waters, plugged in his six-string and launched electrified blues with a series of recordings for *Aristocrat/Chess Records.* His music was heavily adapted from the traditional folk blues handed down to him by older field hands back in Mississippi. He had penned the song *Rollin' Stone* in 1950, when Mick Jagger and Keith Richards were children and more likely dreaming of the tooth fairy than *Jumpin' Jack Flash.* Jagger and Richards' band-mate, Brian Jones, named the band after Muddy's song.

Robert Johnson was another Mississippi bluesman, a contemporary of Waters. Murdered at 27, he didn't live to hear the majority of his two dozen recordings including *When you Got a Good Friend*, *Love In Vain* and *Walkin' Blues*. He died drinking poisoned whiskey planted by a jealous, vengeful husband. His songs have since been proffered by countless messengers of rock and blues, including the Rolling Stones, Eric Clapton, Bonnie Raitt, Johnny Winter and Rory Block, to name only a handful. Listening to *When You Got a Good Friend,* which is virtual rock 'n' roll, one must remind oneself that this dates back to 1937 – almost 20 years before the advent of mainstream rock 'n' roll.

The list of old black blues artists who inspired white post-World War II musicians contains many more names besides Waters and Johnson. Thirteen of 24 (more than half) of the songs on the Rolling Stones' first two albums were either written or first performed by older black American musicians such as Chuck Berry, Bo Diddley, Willie Dixon, Dale Hawkins, and Wilson Pickett (See Appendix IV). The same goes for a dozen songs, or half the material on the Beatles' first two albums.

Much early rock 'n' roll was based on the black twelve-bar blues format, featuring a repeated first line, followed by a wrap-up line. This is exemplified in these well-known lines:

You ain't nothin' but a hound dog, cryin' all the time,
You ain't nothin' but a hound dog, cryin' all the time,
You ain't never caught a rabbit and you ain't no
friend of mine!

Elvis Presley made *Hound Dog* famous in 1955, eclipsing a race recording of the same song two years earlier by Big Mamma Willie Mae Thornton.

Elvis was ahead of his time, as was his then-producer, Sam Phillips. He brought to the bluesy table a handsome white face, a band with drums, back-up singers, and – in white circles, an unprecedented and riveting stage presence. Borrowing heavily from black rhythm and blues, and from gospel music, he found himself piloting the as-yet-not-quite-defined but soon-to-be-skyrocketing milieu of white youth music called rock 'n' roll. White America was not initially accepting of the migration of black music into white performance venues (or into the minds and souls of their children). In Memphis, where he'd launched *Sun Records* to provide recording opportunities for aspiring "colored" musicians, Phillips was called "nigger lover" to his face. In the broader geographic and cultural picture, both Phillips and Presley were initially ostracized, as promoters of vulgarity and evil, by mainstream media and record companies. Aspiring young British musicians, though, were far enough removed from the American dilemma of slavery and the questionable morality and societal value of now-free coloreds. They were unconditionally captivated by songs like Willie Dixon's *Little Red Rooster*, the Isley Brothers' *Twist and Shout*, and Chuck Berry's *Roll Over Beethoven*. White youth music fueled by black forerunners caught on overseas like hell fire. British bands, in particular the Beatles and the Rolling Stones, made the black-to-white musical bridge a seamless non-issue. In the process they made musical history and virtually re-defined England, socially and economically, on the world map.

If this contagious rock music on both sides of the briny was influenced by the Muddy Waters and Robert Johnsons of the 1930s, '40s and '50s, those who elevated the blues from the cornrows of the South, to the streets of the North and eventually the airwaves of the world, who, then, influenced the Muddys and the Roberts? Was there someone before them?

In 1981 I was asking myself this very question.

You know God walked down
in the cool of the day,
And called Adam by his name.
And he refused to answer,
'Cause he was naked and ashamed.

– SON HOUSE

FROM JOHN THE REVELATOR

ROOTS

In 1981, newly divorced, I was trying to support myself as a freelance writer-slash-part-time bookstore clerk-slash-house painter, which often translated to: "Pray for rain and get drunk when it does." My life was in many ways the living blues. Mixed in with regular rejection slips, unpredictable weather and foggy-headed mornings, I listened to the blues, I studied the blues, and I hosted a weekly radio blues program in Rochester, New York. Although I couldn't have articulated it at the time, compiling and broadcasting a blues show featuring an historic and international array of musicians who expressed hurt and self-pity (usually caused in some way by the opposite sex) in the name of art, and in such quantity as to comprise an entire musical genre, gave validity to my own personal pain.

In 1981 I was new to the blues, as well as radio. Presenting an original three-hour, on-air portfolio of blues music, in some way tied together, and on a shoestring budget, took me more than three hours of preparation. I became a forager of sorts. I routinely visited used record stores and dug through forgotten shelves in the public library. There, I ferreted out old blues recordings, on dust-laden black – even red vinyl for my show. I read album liner notes and pored over old music magazine articles on the library microfiche until my head hurt worse than the morning after a rainy day. An extremely territorial homeless man with Tourette's, sporting a Day-glo orange hunting jacket in dire need of laundering, was the only person I know of that spent more time than I in the hidden corners of that library's third floor archives. One day I thought, humorously, of asking him if he'd co-host one show with me, thinking the contrast would be entertaining for the listeners. Over the weeks, though, I came to realize there wasn't much of contrast at all between us. We were both library rats. The only difference was that he didn't need to produce a program broadcasting his condition in order to justify that fact.

I found there were, indeed, musicians who pre-dated Johnson and Waters. One man was mentioned repeatedly by writers, driving home the point that I, myself, didn't even know who my own famous people were. The man continually hailed as a major leg in the journey that brought black music from the southern fields and, through messengers like Johnson and Waters, to the now plugged-in and broadcast music media, had lived right under my nose. He'd lived just across the Genesee River, less than one mile from my Gregory Street apartment, in Rochester, more than a thousand miles from Mississippi, where he'd first made his name – Son House. Son was important to me, but I hadn't realized how important he was in the much bigger picture of music history.

In a 1950s' *DownBeat* magazine interview Muddy Waters stated that the biggest musical influence in his life was Son House. The two had once worked on the same town-sized plantation near Clarksdale, Mississippi. In the 1920s and '30s, Muddy would go to hear Son sing and play in the rural juke joints. One night, armed not with a guitar, but a harmonica, he approached Son between sets and asked if he could join him on stage. House, more than ten years his senior, told him to come back when he was older.

Robert Johnson also grew up in the shadow of Son House. In his book, *Searching for Robert Johnson*, music historian Peter

Guralnick identifies House as Johnson's closest and most direct musical influence. Johnson had a successful albeit brief career as a blues musician, recording in Dallas and performing across the South. He played the open-tuned guitar, like House, and popularized the "walking bass" style of playing, thumbing the low E-string, a defining character of early rock 'n' roll. Johnson's guitar strings were silenced in 1938, the year his womanizing cost him his life. Waters, however, took his voice to Chicago and, playing his electric guitar, also tuned ã la Son House, lived to achieve international fame in his own lifetime.

By the time of Johnson's murder Son House had become a regional singing legend. He had made commercial recordings, but with limited distribution. During this time he was discovered and recorded by John Lomax, and later, John's son, Alan, who were both conducting field studies of authentic American music for the Library of Congress.

Son, however, was not a professional visionary. Unlike Waters, he remained in the Yazoo River Delta Region of Mississippi, contenting himself to plow corn fields, drink corn liquor, and play at juke joints in Mississippi and, occasionally, in Arkansas. Eventually, by the early 1940s, Son had disappeared from the blues radar screen.

Gonna get me religion,
gonna join the Baptist Church
Gonna get me religion,
gonna join the Baptist Church
Gonna be a Baptist preacher
so I don't have to work!

- SON HOUSE
FROM PREACHIN' BLUES

Son House with three blues fans at 61 Greig Street in Rochester.

WATERMAN, VW & CO.

A generation later, 1n 1964, three young blues aficionados, Dick Waterman, Nick Perls and Phil Spiro, captivated by recordings of Son's poignant lyrics, powerful voice and driving guitar, wondered indeed: Whatever happened to Son House? Determined to find out, the friends set out from New York City in a Volkswagen and headed for Memphis, where there'd been a rumored Son House sighting. When that failed to produce the Father of Folk Blues, they went on to rural Mississippi, Son's last known haunt. There the trio drove dirt roads in search of Son House. They walked plowed fields in the scorching sun, and talked to farm workers. They inquired at kerosene-lit shanties at night. They uncovered people who were authentic musicians in their own right, and people who had known Son, but no Son House.

They pushed on and finally found Son, not in the South, but back up north in upstate New York. It was a June day when, after driving four thousand miles through sixteen states chasing false leads Waterman and friends pulled up in front of 61 Greig Street, in the Third Ward neighborhood of Rochester, New York, a very long way from rural Mississippi.

In the album liner notes for *The Legendary Son House: Father of Folk Blues*, which Waterman would soon produce with *Columbia Records*, Waterman describes that day as a warm spring afternoon. He walked up to a man sprawled on the front stoop, a man obviously committed to one major food group: Alcohol.

Waterman eyed him suspiciously, saying, "I'm looking for Son House."

The man worked himself upright, staring at Waterman, and answered in almost question-like form, "I'm him."

How long it had been since Son had sung or played the guitar is unclear, but Waterman began working with him until he was singing and playing the blues with a renewed vigor and a matured voice.

In his 2003 book, *Between Midnight and Day: The Last Unpublished Blues Archive*, Waterman writes:

> After I discovered Son House in June 1964, he appeared at the Philadelphia Folk Festival in late August… (Grammy-winning blues artist) John Hammond was playing at the Gaslite (also in Philadelphia) that weekend.
>
> After Son finished his festival appearance on Sunday afternoon, I decided that we would pay John a visit on our way home to Rochester. The Gaslite was a long, narrow club…
>
> Son and I came into the club, waited until John had finished a song, and…slowly came down the aisle…Then John and I had what must have been one of the shortest conversations in history.
>
> As Son and I moved into the light, John stared at Son, turned towards me, and asked, "Is it?"
>
> "It is," I replied.

Waterman arranged for Son to appear in other festivals, including the 1964 Newport Folk Festival which, amazingly, commenced on July 23, just 29 days after Son's rediscovery. Other performers that year included two rising stars, Joan Baez and Bob Dylan. Son also played in the 1965 New York Folk Festival. Waterman produced Son's aforementioned *'Father of Folk Blues* album, and set up Son on the *American Folk Festival Tour* (in Europe) with Mississippi John Hurt, Skip James, Bukka White, and the blues-driven rock group, Canned Heat. Waterman also coordinated other US and Canadian college and coffee house appearances for Son.

Following the hoopla of Son's rediscovery and during the peak of his amazing comeback, he passed out drunk one winter night on the sidewalk near his home and was covered with snow by a passing city plow truck. He lay there until dawn, when someone found him. As a result of this event Son sustained permanent neurological damage to his left hand and his professional performing days were over. The story of Son House ended again, this time in the mid-1970s. He just up and disappeared.

DEAD OR ALIVE?

By 1981 I had purchased or pirated every known recording of Son House's rich baritone voice. From album jackets and books I had compiled a pretty complete picture of his life, musically. But nowhere did I find the answer to the question: Where is he; what became of Son House, the person?

I found an old poster advertising a Son House performance at the Genesee Co-op Restaurant, on Lower Monroe Avenue. This placed him alive and still in Rochester five years earlier, in 1976. Play It Again Sam was a used record store across the street from the Co-op, where I sometimes purchased albums for my radio show. The manager there was an outgoing, buxom woman. For me, visiting with her was as good a draw on a rainy day as the possibility of finding a newly-arrived blues album. She told me she thought Son House had died. Cancer, she thought. In Florida, she believed. I was disappointed to hear this from her, especially looking as good as she did on that day. Distracted, however, by a streak of good weather and two back-to-back house painting jobs it precipitated, I let the Son House question slide for another month or so. Then one Tuesday night, wrapping up my blues show, listening to my closing theme music – Son's a cappella chant, *Grinnin' in Your Face*, I felt it would be sacrilegious to continue playing this song without knowing what became of the man. I had the last show of the day and was responsible for shutting down the station. Sitting alone in the dark and still studio a few minutes after one o'clock in the morning, I decided I would find that house where he'd lived on Greig Street. The address was in the *'Father of Folk Blues* album liner notes. There might be a clue there; papers left behind; an old neighbor.

The next morning found me staring at an empty space at 61 Greig Street. Son's house was gone. I then recalled something else the manager at Play It Again Sam told me. John Mooney, a young white blues singer from the nearby suburb of Honeoye Falls, had once been close with Son. I'd initially chosen to ignore this information, having ambivalent feelings about younger white men who were overly interested in old black bluesmen. Mooney, though, was now emerging as my only other option.

In a local entertainment publication, *Freetime Magazine*, I found the John Mooney Blues Band was playing that very night, forty miles south of Rochester, at the Naples Hotel. He'd be playing here, in Rochester, in two more days. Even though I'd puzzled over Son's whereabouts – his existence, for more than a year, I now couldn't wait another day. I drove the hour of twisting roads through the Bristol Hills, to Naples, where I cornered Mooney between sets. He was sure Son was alive, living in Detroit. From his guitar case he pulled an address book so old and worn that on the one hand it surely spoke the truth but on the other hand that truth was from another time. Mooney gave me what he believed to be Son's phone number.

Back home, with Son's number written on a bar napkin, I got cold feet. Who knew how long ago Son gave his number to Mooney? He might be dead. Or, if not, he wouldn't want to bother with some guy from Rochester who wanted to meet him and write a story about him. After all he left Rochester behind did he not? Or maybe he would want to see me but then no one would buy my story and I would have let down an old man.

It was four days later, a Monday morning, before I mustered up the courage to pick up the phone. I waited for my two housemates to leave so they wouldn't witness my rejection and disappointment. I dialed the number, expecting to hear a recording: "Your call cannot be completed." People who die in Florida don't generally have active Detroit phone numbers.

A phone started ringing. I paced in the empty kitchen while I waited for someone who never heard of Son House to answer, irritated for having been bothered.

A woman answered.

There's more to a voice than just the measureable tone. There's the guts. There's the attitude. There's the "what-came-before-this-moment in the life of this particular voice." Son House's historic baritone is a perfect example. Then there's his wife. When she answered the phone and heard what I wanted, the initially tentative sound of her hello became quickly the sound of someone who wished she had not answered the phone.

"Yes," she said with an attitude that immediately established she'd already seen and heard it all, she was Son's wife. And yes, he was alive, she admitted. She consented to let me come and interview the 79-year-old blues legend. She reluctantly agreed on a date.

To my "Good-bye," she fired back, "And they don't allow no geetar playin' here!"

ELEVATOR RIDE

On that Saturday in April 1981, when most of the country was preparing to set its clocks ahead an hour, Mark Sampson and I went backward in time. Together we headed out in the rainy dawn for Detroit, to meet Son House.

I'd met Mark at the Village Green Bookstore, another popular Lower Monroe Avenue hub, where I worked part-time, selling magazines, diet soda, cigarettes, candy, novelty hats, and the occasional book. We were introduced to each other by David M., an acquaintance of Mark who worked at the bookstore and knew of our mutual interest in the blues. Mark was the only other Rochesterian I'd met to expend more thought on the question, "Whatever happened to Son House?" than "Hey, let's drink to that!" Mark was a serious amateur photographer and a casual student of the roots of rock 'n' roll. He even owned two steel-bodied acoustic slide guitars, the type that Son had played. They were, in fact, in the back seat of our car, as we drove west out of Rochester, strictly for photographic purposes, of course.

To save time we took a shortcut. Going from Buffalo into Canada, taking the highway through Ontario to Windsor, then crossing the Detroit River into Detroit, is fifty miles shorter in distance than going through Ohio.

We apparently did not appear to be the idealist fans-slash-journalists that we saw when we looked in the mirror. Thanks to a total search of our car and luggage executed by Canadian

Customs at the Canadian border, which including my spare tire compartment and Mark's film canisters – carried out by three Customs personnel, it was about seven hours before we were finally rolling down 3rd Avenue in Detroit.

The marquis on an old theater proclaimed the Bus Boys, America's only all black rock band, were playing there. The fact that they were better known for their *Budweiser* commercial than their opus of creative work, to me, was a reminder of a rift that still existed in this country, between black and white music, seventeen years after the advent of the Beatles and the Stones had presumably erased that line in the sand.

We parked in front of a high-rise housing project and made our way across the front lawn. Surely the whole world could see what we were about. Mark was over six feet and, with his cowboy boots and hat, closer to seven. Carrying a bright red metal guitar, camera and tripod – going to see Son House, he seemed eight feet tall as he proceeded ahead of me down the sidewalk and into the lobby of the high-rise. I followed with the other guitar and backpack full of photo gear. If anyone was against guitar playing in the building, no one, including the two guards at the front door, said a word about our paraphernalia.

Squeezing onto the crowded elevator was like trying to jack up a car while standing up straight. The rest of the people who wanted to use it, most of whom very old and very short, all of whom were black, and none of whom had guitars, seemed adamant about boarding and damned if they were going to be dissuaded by our taking up most of it. On the way up I thought about how Son was discovered in 1930 and recorded by *Paramount Records*. In 1942, John Lomax, folk curator for the Library of Congress, found him and recorded him for the Library. In 1964 Dick Waterman and his friends rediscovered Son living in Rochester. Now the elevator was carrying us up

Columbus' mast to the crow's nest so we could find Son House, the man who'd been discovered more times than America.

We reached the fifth floor and squeezed-shoved-backed our way out of the elevator apologizing to silent, unsympathetic faces. The elevator door slid shut and we stood there in the quiet, dimly lit hallway, staring at Son House's door. We looked at each other.

Mark said, "Well?"

I knocked. The floor was smooth, dark brown, highly waxed linoleum and through the space under the door I could see the shadow of unshod feet silently approach the other side and stop. I straightened myself. This was my very last moment to imagine meeting Son House.

The door opened and a woman in a healthcare worker uniform stood in front of us. I could tell it was the same one who nearly punched me out right through the phone line. She placed herself squarely in the open doorway with her arms folded firmly across her chest.

"What's in it fer him?" she shot at us, before we even got out a "Hello," and in a tone that said she already suspected the answer: Nothing. She looked from me, to Mark, then back at me.

Not expecting outright hostility, it took me a moment to sputter, "Recognition."

Over her unmoving shoulders, a dozen steps behind her, was Son House, facing us, sitting in a La-Z-Boy recliner. His hair was slicked down, his hands rested perfectly on the arms of the chair, his shirt was pressed, he was wearing a tie, and he was smiling – beaming is more accurate. After listening to a couple more of my patronizing observations regarding the value of our visit, Evie House saw there was no way out and let us in on the condition we be brief.

Some got six months, lord, and some a year,
Some got six months, lord, and some a year,
Poor me, poor me got lifetime here.

- SON HOUSE
FROM MISSISSIPPI COUNTY FARM BLUES

Mark Sampson

Gardner and Son House, 1981

"The blues is a low down shakin' chill,
I say, the blues is a low down shakin' chill,
An' if ya'll ain't never had 'em,
I hope you never will."

- SON HOUSE
SON'S BLUES

THE CONTENTS OF APARTMENT #518

The Son House who now faced us did not have the strong, pronounced veins that once stood out in his neck and forehead when he sang – as I'd seen in documentaries and Mark had seen in person. He didn't seem to be retreating inside himself as he did on stage. Nor did he look beyond us, his audience of two, as he often seemed to do when talking on stage, as if he were speaking to someone not in the concert hall but beyond the walls, perhaps back in Mississippi. He was thin, his cheeks were drawn in. I needn't have worried about his tiring of being discovered. He was clearly delighted we had come to see him. He looked directly at us, basking in the outside human contact.

His first words were an apology for having nothing to offer us to drink. His drinking days and performing days, street or stage, were over. Now, five floors above Detroit's 3rd Avenue he vacillated between moments of lucid reflection, to minutes of confusion and a loss for words. Yet I could see in his twinkling eyes the man who jammed with fellow Pre-War blues pioneers, Charley Patton and Willie Brown, toured two continents with Canned Heat, and jammed again in Rochester with a new generation of blues musicians like Joe Beard, John Mooney, and Rockin' Red Palmer. This was clearly the man whose penetrating baritone voice was once known from Mississippi, to Chicago, to London, to local Rochester clubs. This was the man who didn't discriminate between singing the blues and living the blues: excessive drinking, womanizing, panhandling, even pawning his own guitar. He had a spontaneous grin that flashed up and down, from chin to brow. It came and went as he reminisced, patting the arms of the La-Z-Boy, as if wanting to physically re-live those past years.

"I learned to play (guitar) partly from my daddy," said Son. "He was a deacon of the church. He liked to play hymns, not d' blues."

Son had difficulty recalling the names of people and places. He wanted to tell us the name of a bluesman who had influenced him, who, as a young man, he would walk for miles to hear. "The other day I recalled his name to myself..." He was likely referring to either James McCoy, one of the first people Son heard playing the bottleneck-style guitar and from whom Son learned *My Black Mama* and *Preachin' Blues*, or Rube Lacey, then a widely known bottleneck bluesman in the Delta Region.

This rainy Detroit morning, the man who once told Muddy Waters to go away and come back when he was older struggled for answers to my questions; even words. His wife answered a couple questions for him; the names of the countries he'd played in – Austria, England, Canada... following his rediscovery.

Son and Evie married in 1934 but went through periods of separation. Together again now after 47 years of ups and downs, Evie recalled that marriage didn't change anything for Son.

"As soon as we got married, he took off to play in Arkansas. I said, 'That geetar pickin' ain't gonna do you no good!' On the way there he got locked up for a week with Willie Brown."

At the mention of Willie Brown, Son began to discover lost words. "Sometimes we'd (play) Saturday night to sun up. Someone would yell 'Sun up!' and we'd all grab another drink; sometimes even until Sunday evenin'. We'd play until we fell out drinkin' that ol' whiskey. Willie'd be backin' me up…"

"You had to pick up 'n' go to beat Willie," interjected Evie, now smiling, herself. "That was beautiful music."

"After Charlie (Patton) died I was lonely," said Son. "I took a mind to come north with Willie. We had friends in Rochester."

Son and Willie arrived in Rochester in 1943, without Evie. Eventually she would rejoin Son on Greig Street.

"We played some together in Rochester, Willie and I, mostly in homes," said Son.

Willie became quite ill after coming to Rochester and he returned to Mississippi. Shortly after, Son received a letter from Willie's girl. He was dead "of the effects of alcohol."

His friend's death combined with a general Post-War loss of interest in the acoustic, country-style blues, in favor of the newer electric urban blues, caused Son to give up playing.

I was disappointed to see that the apartment was devoid of anything suggesting singing the blues, just plain raising Hell, or even preaching against Hell – Son's one-time other pre-occupation, dabbling in the Baptist ministry. Sure, he had "things," a couch, a chair, but they were just any couch, any chair. There were no concert posters, no photographs of Son posing with Mississippi John Hurt or Canned Heat. There was no tear-stained death letter sitting on a desk, no dusty old walkin' shoes lying in the corner. I panned the room carefully, looking, nay hoping to see a dried ring of whiskey on a table top left from a glass; perhaps a well-thumbed Bible, or an old sepia photograph of hard-faced black deacons standing in front of a rural clapboard church. Instead, a perfectly-folded hand-crocheted afghan and a picture of a grandchild, clearly unenlightened by the blues, smiled brightly back at me. It was as though Son just inhabited this sterile apartment and didn't really "live" here, he was just "doing time" in the latter years of his life.

In fact as he began speaking again I realized he was referring to his music in the past tense: "My blues were about somebody, somethin' real…," he said. "I always liked the meanings of my songs."

As benign as his surroundings appeared, I forced myself to admit, he was surely in better hands, with Evie, than were he left to his own designs.

There was another side of this seemingly sterile environment. Mark and I, as people, were personally present in the apartment. But as blues fans – as fans of this phenomenon no longer seemingly present in Son's life, we and our reason for being here were part of his past. Time, sobriety and Evie had moved Son into a future place, a place further removed from the blues than when he was underemployed, musically silent and virtually invisible for twenty-some years in Rochester, prior to his rediscovery.

I told him we had recently interviewed John Mooney and Joe Beard, back in Rochester. These were two of the last people he'd likely played with. His face brightened. A guitar found its way into his hands. As he began re-adjusting the strings to his favored "open G" tuning, he became mesmerized. His gaze started to drift somewhere else and he appeared to leave us. His whole body stiffened in one mighty effort to strike a chord. But the only sound that came from the guitar was a discordant clunk, the kind you'd expect from someone not accustomed to even handling a guitar. A finger became jammed between the neck and the strings, and he winced. Before Mark or I could step to his rescue, Evie, who, until this point had sat pretty much quietly on the sidelines like a mother watching a child go through an uncomfortable but necessary medical procedure, intervened. Now, both guitars sat silently on the floor. Not instruments of revitalization, but two ships out of water –the Nina and the Pinta of a quest run aground. Painful indicators of how we had disobeyed Evie's request and how our self-serving idealism had undone, rather than summed up the aging Son House's strengths. His physical condition was probably the real "They" Evie had referred to when she'd said, "They don't allow no geetar playin' here!"

The then-recently-released *Tacoma* album, *Rare Blues,* which included Son singing *Preachin' Blues*, at a University of Chicago performance, had just won the 1981 Grammy Award in the category of Ethnic and Traditional Music. I discovered, upon asking, that not even Evie was aware of this. I sensed her reaction of speechlessness was not one of awe, but rather yet another – this one unspoken – "What's in it fer him?!"

The room was silent. Mark had taken his pictures. I could hear through the thin walls a toilet flush in the next apartment. The handwriting leaped off the wall and filled the room: our long-awaited meeting with Son House was over. The 70 years of Son's hell-raising and the 36 years of my tentative existence, culminating in this meeting, was going to be history within the time it took to walk twelve steps back out the door.

As Mark packed his gear and I tried to couch a proper "goodbye," Son slowly leaned forward on the vinyl La-Z-Boy. He mustered up his strength and strung together seven words in a rich and powerful a cappella, "Don'tcha my-yind people grinnin'in yo-ho faaace!" These were lines from the very chant I was using to open and close my blues program. I recalled, then, something John Mooney had told us: Son never sang or played the blues in the house. His wife wouldn't allow it. Son had just crossed the line for us. And himself.

It looked like 10,000 people standin'
'round the burying ground,
It looked like 10,000 people standin'
'round the burying ground,
I didn't know I loved her
'til they begun to let her down.

- SON HOUSE
FROM DEATH LETTER BLUES

CORPOREAL PERFORMANCE

Following our meeting with Son House, Mark and I decided to catch an early dinner before heading home. We wound up in a very a nice restaurant in a Downtown Detroit hotel, a far cry from Son's small, stark, yet intimate space. Here we invested some of our anticipated journalistic profits in fine dining and beverages.

Darkness was falling as we crossed the bridge from Detroit, into Windsor, Ontario, and began the shortcut through Canada, back to Buffalo and then Rochester. Mark stuffed a tape in the deck, turned the volume up and, in less than ten kilometers, was asleep. Neil Young was wailing, "Hey, hey, my, my; rock and roll will never die. It's better to burn out, than it is to rust..."

Spurred by wine-induced confidence and under the guiding hand of Saint House, protector of impaired travelers, this minor league freelance journalist drove into the dark, foggy night, through rural Canada, passing signs for turn-offs to London, then Paris, Ontario. I thought of Son House; imagined how he might still be singing – maybe as a star, like Muddy Waters, in that spine-chilling voice, laying down blues riffs on his steel-bodied acoustic guitar, laying down rows of goose bumps on the flesh of men and women alike, if he hadn't compromised his options with booze.

When Son was still performing, Dick Waterman (who accompanied him to all his performances) told a blues critic,

"I've been everywhere with him and at every performance I am still tremendously moved by this man as an artist."

Describing Son's 1967 appearance at the De Montford Hall in Leicester, England, where he performed with Canned Heat, Bob Groom wrote in *Blues World* magazine:

> It's difficult to describe the transformation that took place as this smiling, friendly man hunched over his guitar and launched himself, bodily it seemed, into his music. The blues possessed him like a 'lowdown shaking chill' and the spellbound audience saw the very incarnation of the blues as, head thrown back, he hollered and groaned the disturbing lyrics and flailed the guitar, snapping the strings back against the fingerboard to accentuate the agonized rhythm. Son's music is the centre of the blues experience and when he performs it is a corporeal thing, audience and singer become as one.

In much fewer words, Rochester blues guitarist, Aleks Disljenkovic, who had known and heard Son, said, "Son House's voice was so powerful he didn't need a PA system, his voice would pin you to the wall."

It likely was that very "pin-you-to-the-wall-slash-corporeal" phenomenon that, in the 1920s and 30s, drew in and made believers – nay, avid disciples, of Muddy Waters and Robert Johnson. I had just experienced this pin-you-to-the-wall power, myself, earlier. Son's grin, just his presence, had caused me to feel that "There's no agenda; everything's okay right now, because nothing else exists or matters, just 'us' and 'now.'"

I crossed the international Peace Bridge at around 3:00

A.M., leaving behind London and Paris, and entering New York State's western gem, Buffalo, and the US. I was yawned across the US border without incident by a night worker, a very young woman who might have been a coed from one of the nearby universities. I followed the New York State Thruway east for seventy-five miles, and reached Rochester with a foggy pre-dawn now in the air, but with a strangely clear head, and very much in the "now."

Oh, a brown-skinned woman
will make a rabbit move to town,
Oh, a brown-skinned woman
will make a rabbit move to town,
Oh, but a real black woman'll
make a mule kick his stable down.

-SON HOUSE
FROM MY BLACK MAMA PART II

CORNROW VII:
REFLECTING

Mark and I drove to Detroit to show Son our appreciation. We had hoped to raise him from obscurity and give him some deserved but long overdue recognition, particularly among the citizens of Rochester, where he lived, however invisibly, for more than three decades, longer than any other place he called home. We could do that now. We could tell his story.

I'd also selfishly thought if only I could meet Son House – speak to him, I would, somehow be rescued from my own life. He could sing his blues, but I couldn't sing mine. I needed him to sing me, for me. I could then hopefully become savvy to and a survivor of the world of, among other things, lost love, loneliness and depression. I would have peace. In his autobiographical novel, *A Fan's Notes*, Frederick Exley talks about the first time he had his heart broken by a woman. He "…became an English major with a view to reading the books, the novels and the poems – those pat assurances that other men had experienced rejection, pain and loss…"

I now realized Son House wasn't performing the blues as much as living them. He just happened to be able to sing about his life, poetically, passionately and publicly, to articulate it for others who also lived, but perhaps couldn't express life. One could earn a master's degree in guitar performance yet still not be able to convey what Son could convey with his dirty fingernails, worn out guitar, three-chord compositions and virtually no formal education. Son was the reason for the guitar. He was the instrument. He was the very reason for blues to be sung. When he played he was everything, the message, the instrument, even me and the rest of the audience. My own needs and expectations of our visit blinded me from the possibility that he needed me, or us – his fans – people, as much as we him. He had the music within him and he had to share it.

There is another reason I went to Detroit. An odd parallel of sorts existed between two very unlikely people in my life: Eddie J. "Son" House, Jr., personable alcoholic, Baptist minister-turned-bluesman, and Hiram Edgar Shade, musician-turned-Baptist minister and strict, foreboding teetotaler.

The latter was my grandfather. Not to be confused with my own children's 'Grandpa at the Beach' to whom this book is dedicated. Hiram thought children should be seen and not heard. My grandfather was probably ten years older than Son. He never spoke to me, not once, not even by accident, in the seven years we co-occupied this planet, including the summers I remember my parents, my brother and I sharing with him in a four-room cottage on Keuka Lake. He was tall for his generation and looked down, literally, at almost everyone around him. If my grandfather had been frivolous enough to brandish a bumper sticker, it would never have said "Happiness is being a grandparent." It could, though, have said, "I prefer fishing over family; a biting trout is better than an ankle-biting grandchild," or maybe, "I am a heartless German prick; ask my grandchildren."

I don't know if he was always like this. There was no discussing it. His own children – my mother and her two sisters – were afraid to talk about him. As a young man Hiram started out, like Son, in manual labor, in his case working not in the cotton and corn fields of Mississippi, but in a Pittsburgh saw mill. Like Son played the juke joints of the Yazoo River Delta region, Hiram played the fiddle, performing in bars and taverns in and around that famous steel city where the Monongahela and Allegheny Rivers converge to form the Ohio River. One day there was an accident at the mill. Mr. Warm & Fuzzy lost two fingers on his left hand.

Jumping ahead for a moment to one summer at the cottage when I was five or six and my grandfather was still alive: He had come into the kitchen at breakfast-time from his daily pre-dawn lake trolling.

Seeing the size of his fish, my mother said, "Dad, please show Richie your fish."

My grandfather held out something on a piece of newspaper.

"Dad, you have to bend down so he can see them."

He stooped over and my gaze was frozen first on the wide open eyes of two fish, each a good 18 inches long. Then my gaze fell on his two missing fingers, now just stumps. I was transfixed by the sight of the bones in the stumps. They moved visibly under the skin in unison with his other fingers. The accident ended his fiddle playing and his job at the mill. So he became a Baptist Minister. The man who'd once played the Devil's music in bars now preached against it. He became a teetotaler. And not just against alcohol. The Accidental Minister now saw even Coca-Cola as an evil of the flesh. And candy, and dancing, and television. And children who were heard when they should in fact only be seen.

One day at the cottage when he, my mother and I were together in the small living room. He spoke to my mother about me in the third person, "That child sure talks a lot."

My mother's response was apologetic. Hiram was apparently a hit with his colleagues, though. He became President of the Baptist Minsters Association of Western Pennsylvania. But his dark, almost punitive shadow rained a strange and negative mist on our family that lasted for decades, starting with his own wife, then his children – my mother and her two sisters, and finally worked its way down to my brother and me. He pressured my mother, at 19, to drop out of voice lessons, convincing her that opera, her chosen field, was worldly and not something Jesus would want her to do. In retrospect I can see this left her repressed and depressed. As a result, although my brother and I grew up in an intellectually stimulating environment, there was an emotional and spiritual void. I, like my mother, believed my grandfather's way was the right way and that my ultimate rejection of it meant that there was something wrong with me, not him. He was my grandfather, after all, was he not? Even if he wouldn't talk to me. And she was my mother. I quit high school in the tenth grade due in no small part to this inherited intolerance on my mother's part, for the things I wanted to do. After all, I was surely going to Hell. Why bother with homework? I wouldn't need a diploma there. My brother followed suit in eleventh grade.

So my grandfather started out in the bars and wound up in the Baptist pulpit. Son started out attempting the calling of the Baptist pulpit, but eventually gave in to the Devil's music, and to the bars and the life that went with it. They both experienced a spiritual 180. Son in an unassuming way; my grandfather in a forced way. I wanted – no, needed to meet this man who not only went 180 degrees against my grandfather's will and my family's beliefs, but who had the audacity to write and record a song about it.

From Son's Preachin' Blues:

> *"Gonna get me religion, gonna join the Baptist Church;*
> *Gonna be a Baptist preacher, so I don't have to work."*

I would eventually, upon leaving the protective confines of my parents' house and going out on my own, realize there were opportunities in life independent of the religious framework that shaped my first two decades. I would re-join forces with the educational system and graduate from college. But discovering Son, his rejecting of the religion of my grandfather and going the way of the blues was a milestone in my life. It provided me with a sense of validity in some of the choices I'd made. Only time will tell if Hiram's *Holy Bible* or Son's Mississippi National resonator guitar spoke the bigger truth.

THE WRATH OF A WOMAN IGNORED

Upon our return from Detroit, I wrote a story about finding Son House for *Upstate Magazine*, the Sunday rotogravure of the Rochester *Democrat & Chronicle*. Far from not being interested, as I'd once feared, the editors made it the cover story. I was hosting my weekly blues show on WGMC-FM and in the by-line of the article it was mentioned I would be airing a special program on Son House on the show, that coming Tuesday.

For the story, I had also interviewed Rochester bluesman, John Mooney, twenty-something, who, as a white suburban teenager, had followed Son around, drinking cheap whiskey, panhandling, visiting pawn shops, and performing in local bars and coffee houses – learning the blues first-hand from the greatest folk bluesman still alive. Mooney, by now an established professional musician agreed to come on my Son House special and play three songs, live. I thought my 10-year-old daughter, Amy, would appreciate being part of a radio broadcast that included a live performance, even it weren't Blondie or Joan Jett & the Blackhearts. I arranged with my ex-wife, Amy's mom, to let her help me on the show. I had not done a broadcast involving a live performance so I had worked it out with the station manager that I would arrive a half-hour before airtime so he could show me how to set up the studio mikes for Mooney.

When Amy and I arrived, I found that the manager, a man with even less depth in real life than suggested by his contrived radio name and vapid on-air personality, had put the station on "automatic play" and was walking out the door, headed for home.

He said, "There's somebody waiting for you in the studio, she's got something to show you."

This struck me as odd; no one was allowed in the studio except the on-air person.

I raised my eyebrows, "'Someone?'"

"Oh," he said, "It's Canny P, our Saturday folk music program host."

My daughter and I carried our load of vinyl albums into the anteroom, the last cubicle before the on-air studio. There sat a woman holding an old metal resonator guitar similar to the one Mark had brought to Detroit for Son to play. This one was dented and worn to the bare metal in several places. "Hi, Rich," she said, occupying the only seat in the room and not getting up, "I'm Canny P..."

Before I could respond she continued, "Do you know what this is?" She held the guitar in one hand by its neck and thrust it toward me as if it were a cross and I a vampire.

I said, "A Mississippi National..."

"It's Son House's guitar," she interrupted in a tone that had changed completely from the "Hi, Rich" of a moment ago.

"I followed him into a pawn shop in 1974," she continued, "and bought it back after he sold it! He kept pawning it and I kept buying it back."

She was leaning forward, now, and raising her voice to me in a tone that even my daughter recognized as not right between two adults who have only just met.

"Finally I kept it, and I've been playing it ever since!"

At this, I now recognized her name not just from the list

of program hosts here at the station, but as a name I'd once heard in connection with the local circuit of folk singers.

"I want to know why you didn't interview me for that article," she virtually demanded. "You interviewed John Mooney!"

The way his name rolled off her lips told me she was definitely not a fan of John Mooney.

"…and Joe Beard! But you never even…"

I interrupted, "Your name never came up. I'm sorry, I had no intention of leaving anyone out…"

She was barely in control of her anger, and proceeded there in front of my daughter to denigrate the playing ability and moral character of John Mooney. Air time was approaching. I had mikes to set up, albums to stage, and commercials to review. All I could think was: How do I get this woman out of here?

The onus of this task was taken from me by none other than John Mooney. In the front door he walked, wearing a big smile, carrying a shiny new chrome-plated guitar, and holding hands with a svelte young woman. They were unaware of the confrontation I was in.

Mooney showing up at the station, obviously to play on the air for the Son House special, was the last straw for Canny. She stood, brushed past us all without a word, and carried herself and Son's guitar out the door.

Growing up in America, I had been inclined to attribute extra intelligence, knowledge, a sense of accountability and even power to those who spoke to the masses: a high school principal reading the Honor Roll over the school's PA system; a football stadium announcer; a newscaster or program host on radio or television. As I was learning, this wasn't necessarily the case, at least not here, not tonight.

It was in particular not the case of the station manager, whose interest in, and accountability for radio station operations, seemed to begin and end with hearing the sound of his own voice over the airwaves. He had left without showing me how to hook up my live music broadcast. Mooney bailed me out for a second time; he knew how to set up the mikes and went to work on it.

This confrontation had not helped my mental state. I was thankful to have my daughter with me so I could explain to her how to cue commercials and how to stage records on the dual turntables. Mooney set up opposite us on the other side of the glass, in the other half of the studio. He did a sound check and gave me a thumbs up through the glass; we were ready.

Airtime: I cued a station break, then activated my mike and we were live. I explained that we were doing a Son House special; we'd play three Son recordings and then be treated to some live music by Son House protégé – Rochester's own, John Mooney. I played the three Son House cuts, did a commercial, and went right to Mooney. He was dynamic; it was obviously worth the trouble to set up this live broadcast. I watched him through the glass as he belted out his version of Son's *Pony Blues*, and slid that metal piece along the neck of his open-tuned guitar, a la Son House. Suddenly a faint image appeared standing next to Mooney…the ghost of Son House? No, Son was alive and in Detroit. Was it the ghost of Willie Brown, back from the dead, to accompany, at least in spirit, his old blues partner?

Whoever it was, he was wearing a hat; a policeman's hat. It was not a ghost. It was a reflection in the glass that separated me from Mooney. A policeman had come into the studio and was standing behind me. I turned and looked up at him.

"There's been a bomb threat, you have to close up and get out."

"A bomb threat?" I asked, "Surely you're kidding!"

He shook his head.

I thought: This is a Tuesday evening in conservative Rochester, New York. A 'bomb?' I'll bet there isn't even an illegal firecracker in the whole County. And besides, I'm doing a Son House special program, I don't care if there's a real bomb.

The officer's response to my not moving was calm but firm, "You have to leave, immediately. Announce on the air that 'broadcasting is being shut down due to technical difficulties,' then shut down whatever you have to, and get all of these people out of here, right now."

Disbelief turned to frustration. I was momentarily unable to move as I thought of all the work that went into this: dragging Mooney in here, having my ex-wife bring my daughter 40 miles into the city – keeping her out of school tomorrow, and getting the editor of *Upstate Magazine* to plug the show; not to mention the original intent of the show, to give Son House some long overdue recognition. Now, it was all down the drain. Two police officers waited for us; me, my daughter, Mooney and his lady friend – to walk out with them.

As we were collecting our gear, one of the officers asked me, "Do you know anyone who would call in a bomb threat?"

"No," I responded.

"Has anyone left here angry in the last hour?" he pressed.

Without thinking, I said "No!" Then, "Wait a minute, was it a woman's voice that called it in?"

The officer nodded. I told them what happened, almost apologetically, because I was embarrassed and angered by how Canny had reduced us here at the station to what probably appeared to these cops as a bunch of quarreling children. Now knowing who the caller surely was and that there wasn't a bomb, didn't change anything; we still had to shut down. We closed the door on Son House's three-hour special less than fifteen minutes into it.

When I called the station manager the next day, to tell him what happened, he claimed to know nothing about it and appeared as concerned as if I were reporting a broken chair. He said he'd talk to Canny, but doubted whether she would have been responsible for anything like that. There was no follow-up of any kind that I know of on the part of the police or the station management, either on the bomb threat or my allegations of who the perpetrator likely was.

UNCANNY AFTERMATH

I left the radio station about six months after the bomb threat. A year or so after my departure, Grammy Award-winning blues musician, John Hammond came to Rochester to play at a local nightclub, the Red Creek Inn. I had played John's music regularly on my show and still listened to him at home. I was up in the air about whether to spend the money to go see him live until I discovered that Canny P was opening for him. Could the one and only bomb-threatening Canny possibly be good enough to open for an artist of this caliber? I decided to go, even though my purchase of a ticket, I realized, would be supporting the aspirations of a woman who not long ago undermined my own aspirations, and in an underhanded and illegal way.

I arrived early at the 'Creek' and was one of just a handful of people near the stage watching at the beginning of Canny's set. There she was, the woman who pulled the plug on a radio program and deprived an old bluesman of some long overdue public recognition. Ha! – here was the woman whose ass, for two years, had warmed the exact same chair as mine – at the radio station controls – but on a different day. When I was looking for people who had known Son House, to interview, she was, ironically, unknown to me.

There she was now, walking to the chair at the mike with the old and worn guitar that was once Son's; the one from the night of the bomb scare.

I wondered if she knew I was there. When you hate someone with passion – as she did me – does that passion give you extrasensory powers?

I thought of ducking out to the lobby, calling in a bomb threat from the pay phone, and causing the place to be evacuated. But I couldn't bring myself to do something that rash. Besides, Jeff, the owner of the establishment, had been the sponsor of my blues show; he wouldn't have appreciated a stunt like that.

When she finally began playing I was taken aback. I'd never then or since heard a woman channel so much anger through voice and instrument. She seemed to leave the audience and go away to another place, very much like Son House used to do when he performed. I wondered if she had perhaps shared more with Son House than his metal instrument. Her voice wailed and she snapped – beat the guitar strings in a manner I found more disquieting than cool. I, another man, and the woman he was with stood, almost simultaneously, and walked to the bar on the other side of the club, where we sat and self-medicated for the remainder of her set.

She's got a mean old fireman
and a lowdown engineer.
She's got a mean old fireman
and a lowdown engineer.
She's taken my baby away from me
and left me standin' here.

- SON HOUSE
FROM EMPIRE STATE EXPRESS

CORNROW X:
EPITHET

On October 19, 1988, seven-and-a-half years after Mark and I drove to Detroit that rainy spring Saturday to interview Son House, the Father of Folk Blues disappeared for the last time, quietly, in Detroit's Harper Hospital, unaccompanied by music, whiskey, or blues fans. There is, among music historians, some disagreement as to Son's date of birth, however, the most oft-cited is March 21, 1902. This would have made him eighty-six years and seven months old.

In spite of a hard lifestyle, Son outlived, by a combined total of 80 years, four important young musicians with whom he was associated: his two notable progeny, Robert Johnson (1911 to 1938) and Muddy Waters (1915 to 1983), and the two front men in Canned Heat, Alan Wilson (1943 to 1970) and Robert Hite (1945 to 1981).

John Mooney, the young bluesman who gave me Son's phone number and played at the radio station, has evolved into a nationally-recognized, award-winning musician. At this writing, he's front man for the New Orleans-based band, Bluesiana. Mooney's guitar technique and vocal – including moaning, on his version of Son's *Pony Blues* is Son House re-incarnate.

Following his rediscovery of Son House in 1964, Dick Waterman launched Avalon Productions, dedicated to promoting and managing blues musicians, many of whom, like Son, had slipped into obscurity. He re-introduced the likes of

Arthur Crudup, Lightnin' Hopkins, Mississippi John Hurt, J.B. Hutto, Skip James, Junior Wells, Bukka White and, of course Son, to a whole new young and receptive audience. He went on to discover and manage Bonnie Raitt, and was the promoter of Bob Dylan's 1975-76 Rolling Thunder Review tour, featuring a lineup of folk-country musicians. Waterman's book, *Between Midnight and Day: the Last Unpublished Blues Archive,* is a must-read collection of stories and photographs, historically and artistically important, of the musicians he worked with or met during his decades on the road. Included in the book are vignettes about Son and some outstanding photos of Son. When Waterman writes about Muddy Waters he tells of a young member of Waters' band waiting in the wings, at Carnegie Hall, to go on stage. The young man was making fun of a funny old man, Son House, also waiting to perform. Waters called the kid on it, saying, "If it weren't for that 'old man' we wouldn't be here right now."

I spoke with Dick Waterman in 2004. He told me, "Royalties for Son's music are finally coming in, to Son's daughter. Too bad Son couldn't have seen some of this."

Nick Perls, one of those accompanying Dick Waterman in 1964, when they found Son living in Rochester, was obsessed with old blues music. He knocked on doors of individual homes throughout the South and searched pawn shops and used record stores in Northern cities for old recordings. By the late 1960s he had amassed such a large number of rare and obscure recordings that he launched *Yazoo Records*, dedicated to converting old recordings, usually 78 rpm shellac originals, to 33 rpm discs. Thanks to his interest in authentic American music and his spirit of entrepreneurship a vast body of original music, and the voices of those who performed it, is available to the public; music that otherwise would have been gone forever. Perls died of AIDS in 1987 and *Yazoo Records* was acquired by *Shanachie Records.*

Whatever became of Canny P, bomb-scare artist? ("Canny" is an anagram of her real name) That's one blues artist I'd rather not rediscover.

Son House in his home at 61 Greig Street in Rochester. Tuning a visitor's guitar to "Open G."

Photo (1974) Warren H. Zuelke, Jr.

CORNROW XI:
WALKING THROUGH HISTORY ONE E-STRING AT A TIME

I decided to honor Son privately on his 110th birthday by visiting his ghost. March 21, 2012, I drove to the west side of the Genesee River, near downtown Rochester. I parked and found my way on foot to the site where Son's third floor walk-up once sat on Greig Street. Today, the building is gone and so is the street, at least the block on which Son lived. Greig Street runs only from Lunsford Circle Park to Clarissa Street. In Son's time it continued across Clarissa, ending at the intersection of Ford and Exchange Streets. Today, if you ignore the fact that Greig Street ends, and continue walking south, past Clarissa, on the sidewalk alongside the RL Edwards Manor senior living facility, you'll come to a large brick office building whose front door reads "Rochester Correctional Facility." Constructed in 1905, it was once the convent for the nearby Immaculate Conception Church. On old plat maps it is identified as #55 Greig Street. Since Greig Street is now gone, the building has adopted, for its address, 470 Ford Street (Ford runs behind it). Where the flag poles are in the parking lot to the south of the building is where Son's house once sat; #61 Greig Street. Old maps show two more buildings, #63 and #67 tucked into that space before the street ended at Ford and Exchange.

Windsor Wade and I worked together at Hillside Children's Center in the late 1970s. Today he's a social studies teacher at the Rochester City School District's School Without Walls. In the mid-1970s, before we met, he had come back from a stint in Vietnam, and was a graduate student at SUNY Brockport. During this time he worked for a semester in that brick building – then as now, a halfway house for recently released prisoners – directly next door to Son's house.

"Coming to work one day, I saw this guy sitting on the front porch of the house next door," said Windsor. "I knew who Son House was and thought that might be him. I looked up a picture of him and thought, 'Holy s---, that is Son House!' I introduced myself to him and shook his hand. From that point on, if he was out there, he'd say, 'Hey, young fella!' – He didn't remember my name – and I'd stop and shake his hand. He was never playing a guitar, just sunning himself. Most of the time he was in no condition to be playing," Windsor added, making light humor of Son's drinking.

At SUNY Brockport Windsor met a student from New York City who was into the blues."I told him, 'Son House lives next door to where I work.' He says, 'Are you serious?!'

"I brought him with me one day and he met Son. After that he continued to visit Son.

"Other people would find out where he lived, too, and would come to visit him." Windsor clarified, "They were all white, always white."

Themselves, part of the black migration, Windsor's family had come north, in his case from Florida, to Rochester, in search of a better quality of life. Here they were disappointed to find an invisible, but clearly drawn color line in the city.

"My mother wouldn't have any part of that," Windsor said, "so we moved to Holley."

His father got a job at Duffy-Mott; his mother began college and eventually became a nurse.

Windsor had an uncle who was an itinerant musician and had lived a somewhat hard life. So he spoke from personal experience when he said of Son, "I used to think, 'What a shame, seeing him out there on his front porch in that condition, with all that talent.' That's just one of the tragedies that can occur, being a man and being black."

Standing in front of Son's missing house now, on his 110th birthday, I thought I would like to see a designated space in the Rochester Correctional Facility parking lot. Near the front door, next to the parking space for handicapped drivers with its stenciled wheelchair logo. I'd like to see a space with a sign that read, "Reserved for the possible re-appearance, yet again, of Son House, Father of Folk Blues, and arguably the most influential person, however overlooked, to inhabit this neighborhood, now called Corn Hill, in all of recorded history." The outline of a Mississippi National steel-bodied acoustic guitar could be stenciled on the asphalt parking space.

I am not the only blues fan who wonders at the lack of recognition for Son House. Gary Wooten, one-time lead singer for the blues band, the Trendsetters, once said to his audience between songs during a set at the nearby blues and jazz club, Clarissa's, "You know, one of the greatest bluesmen there ever was lived just down the street from here?!"

I personally experienced this neighborhood in the 1960s, the decade of Son's rediscovery here by Dick Waterman and friends. The city was divided into Wards and in those days. This was called the Third Ward. Rochester Institute of Technology (RIT) was located nearby in the Plymouth Avenue-West Broad Street area, abutting the Ward. Hundreds of college students lived in the Ward's stately 19th-century homes, broken up into rentable rooms and apartments. Greek fraternity letters, bigger than parking spaces, were painted in the street with wide brushes and house paint. Draft beer was the unofficial beverage. There was no expressway, yet, cutting through this part of town. Students could walk from the Ward, down Washington Street, to the bars, coffee houses (and, incidentally, their classes) on West Broad, or cross the river, on foot, on the Troup-Howell Bridge, to the night life on Lower Monroe Avenue. The drinking, painting, studying students shared this neighborhood with another group of citizens, sardined into these streets and homes alongside them, urban blacks. For years the two groups coexisted like tap water and olive oil, without friction, but also without mixing.

I was a suburban teenager in the 1960s. The Ward was my first exposure to college students. Many of them were still teenagers who lived in this seemingly miraculous dream world apart from their parents. A world that included, besides beer, cohabitating with girlfriends and boyfriends, sleeping in mornings, macaroni-and-cheese for breakfast, lunch and dinner, and not having to shower daily (not necessarily all at one time). And the scholars appeared none the worse for it. And it was my first exposure to blacks, who also seemed to live in another world, one of quiet acceptance. I knew nothing, then, about Son House or the genre of blues music. One of the first things an RIT student might learn was on which door to knock when you ran out of alcohol and the liquor stores were closed. A few students were kind enough to pass along this information about extra-curricular collegiate activities, tuition-free, to those of us attending their impromptu parties in the Ward.

My cross-cultural Baptism occurred, therefore, at the same time and in the same place as my introduction to college life. In the '60s liquor stores weren't open on Sundays. One

Sunday afternoon in the Ward I walked, as directed, down a dozen concrete stairs and made an exchange with a sixty-something black man standing in his basement doorway, somewhere near the intersection of Atkinson and Eagle Streets. I handed him the equivalent of an hour's pay from my after-school job at Wolf's Delicatessen, and he handed me a pint of vodka. I noticed the seal was broken and realized it was probably watered down but, I reasoned, this must be the unwritten rule for under-the-table Sunday liquor sales. The transaction, itself, was equivalent to nothing I'd participated in prior. I was under-aged. The sale and the purchase were both illegal. To boot, coming from a strict religious household, the alcohol made it a sin, no matter what day of the week, or how old I was. The man, however, appeared as moral in persona and as comfortable with his mortal destination as anyone I'd met in my parent's church.

There is a major historical phenomenon that coincided with the discovery of Son House living in the Ward, one which my teenage friends and I were well aware of. Although not connected to his discovery, it cannot be ignored in telling this story because it couches the societal framework within which Son existed and in which his re-discovery took place.

Waterman and friends found Son on June 23, 1964. Thirty-one days later – on July 24 – a series of events occurred in Rochester that would impact the nation and would be a major precursor in addressing the inter-racial face of America. On that day Rochester police were called to an inner-city party involving underage drinking. The party was in the Eighth Ward, in Rochester's northeast quadrant. The Third Ward, in which Son lived, was in the southwest quadrant. The police allegedly over-reacted in responding and used excessive force, including the use of a police dog. Since the youths were black and the vast majority of the police at that time were white, the ensuing clash between partiers and cops was dubbed a race riot. The rioting would spread to other parts of the city and continue for three days, spilling into other neighborhoods and, finally, into the Third Ward. A man was killed near the intersection of Atkinson and Clarissa Streets, only a few hundred steps from the sunny front stoop of our smiling, friendly bluesman.

While the riots were reported by some media as directly related to the police action, other reports suggested the riots had less to do with the one-time teenage party and more to do with a long and quiet simmering of urban blacks, struggling for years with invisible color lines, finally coming to a boil. At the end of three days, four people were dead, 350 had been injured, 1000 people had been arrested, and over 200 (mostly white-owned) stores and businesses had been looted or damaged.

The Rochester riots would spark national attention. Race riots erupted 60 days later in Philadelphia, the following summer in the Watts Neighborhood of Los Angeles, then the Hough Neighborhood in Cleveland; then in Detroit, Newark, Minneapolis-St. Paul, and other cities. More than 100 people would die, thousands would be injured and thousands more arrested; property damage would be staggering; in Detroit, alone, 2,000 buildings were destroyed. "Civil Rights" would become a household word. The activism of Martin Luther King, Jr., and others, would become a daily news staple.

It is tragically ironic that this national violence associated with the inability to tolerate color lines any longer coincided with a resurging interest, nationally – in fact internationally, in these very lines. An interest that manifested itself in the form of a new receptiveness of younger and, yes, white audiences waiting to hear the likes of Son House and a handful of his surviving contemporaries who had also been rediscovered. Son

House was, in fact, performing before an international audience, at the Newport Folk Festival, thirty days after his re-discovery, the very same weekend the riots were occurring in Rochester.

My Sunday afternoon transactions of watered-down pints of vodka were not affected by Rochester's four deaths and 1,000 arrests. Getting toasted on a Sunday afternoon was not a socio-political statement. It was a matter of pleasure and economics, factors that have always seemed to win out in our culture, personally and nationally. And those basement door exchanges were, indeed, actions, not words. He and I rarely spoke. They became a virtual tradition, for as long as my friends and I were unable to put aside enough on Saturday night, of that which we would surely want on hand for Sunday.

When, nearly two decades later, I was finally confronted with and arrested by the voice of Son House, my reaction was not based on who he was (a black man) or where he had lived (right under my nose). The voice of Son House was a figurative hand that pulled me out of a well of sorrow and self-pity I'd fallen into following my divorce and my inability to look in on my children each night as they slept, simply to make sure they were there.

During part of the time he lived in the Third Ward, Son worked for the New York Central Railroad as a porter. He wrote *Empire State Express*, which he recorded on his 1965 *Father of Folk Blues album*, for *Capitol Records*. On that track Canned Heat's Al Wilson backed him on second guitar. Son wound up living in Rochester for over thirty years, most of that on Greig Street, longer than any other individual place in his 86 years.

In 1968 RIT relocated to the suburb of Henrietta, a long planned move reportedly not directly related to the riots. In the aftermath there was, in the void created, confusion about the direction of this once busy and highly purposeful neighborhood

– that purpose being the rental of poorly-maintained housing to college students and marginalized blacks. Many now vacant homes – former student quarters – for years neglected by absentee landlords, were torn down. Son's was one of them. The indiscriminate razing of structures displaced most of the remaining residents (blacks), but also began attracting urban homesteaders (predominately white) from outside the neighborhood. They saw beauty in the stately old homes and narrow 19th-century streets. And they saw value as well, since one could pick up a house in this virtually condemned neighborhood for as little as the price of a car. The newcomers began rehabilitating the salvageable homes and many razed houses were replaced with new town homes. The gentrified neighborhood was renamed Corn Hill, a name once associated with this area by Rochester's first settlers.

Were a designated parking space created for Son House, he probably wouldn't use it, even if he were alive. Although he was a respected tractor operator in the South (when he lived in Mississippi he was once released from prison, for shooting a man, because his plantation boss wanted him back on the tractor), he didn't drive when he came north. He walked everywhere. On his 2003 posthumously-released *New York Central Live* CD he talks about walking down Plymouth Avenue, in the Third Ward, in the 1940s and '50s, and passing another New York Central porter, Lattimore, who also worked part-time for an undertaker.

Son says on the CD, "Here come Lattimore again, drivin' along tootin' his horn, and I cut my eyes away. He owns a Cadillac and drives a hearse – that's two 'dead wagons' – an' I'm still walkin!'"

One place he might have been "walkin'" was Shep's Paradise, a nearby bar in Son's day. So I decide to walk it on his birthday, and count my steps – Son's steps. I walk 160 steps, about 400 feet, north from Son's former front door, to Clarissa Street. I turn left and walk along Clarissa. I pass the Memorial AME Zion Church, the Mt. Olivet Baptist Church, and the First Church of God. It's ironic that Son might have passed so many churches on his way to a bar. His walking along this route would have been a metaphor for his life, during which he wrestled back and-forth with religion, the blues and alcohol choosing at one point to be a Baptist preacher, then leaving the church in favor of the juke joints and roadhouses of the South.

Shep's was once a hangout for blues and jazz musicians, black and white, including Grammy-winning jazz-pop composer and flugelhorn player, Chuck Mangione, his brother, jazz pianist and composer, Gap Mangione, and John "Spider" Martin, Jr., a saxophonist (1931-2000) who played with many headliners including Lionel Hampton, Dizzy Gillespie, Tony Bennett and Aretha Franklin. Shep's Paradise later became the Clarissa Room and at this writing is now simply Clarissa's.

The distance from Son's house to Clarissa's turns out to be a cool one thousand footsteps, or about half-a-mile. I figure two-and-a-half feet per step. My stride is probably a bit longer than Son's, since I'm a bit taller than he was. I'd estimate his stride was about 30," or about the length of the high E-string on a Mississippi National steel-bodied acoustic guitar, the repeated snapping of that string being one of Son's trademarks.

For a moment I allow myself to think that I just walked Son's walk. But no one can walk Son's walk, not even one that lasts only ten minutes and involves no music. Only he can walk it, and he surely did.

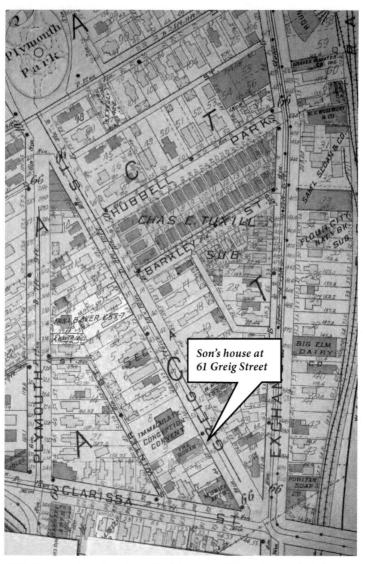

1918 plat map shows location of Son's house at 61 Greig Street. Greig Street runs almost perfectly north and south. Until the 1970s, Greig Street reached all the way from the Plymouth Park traffic circle, to the Clarissa Street Bridge. Clarissa and Ford Streets were re-routed. The bridge is now the Ford Street Bridge.

61 Greig Street, where Son House lived from 1943 through the early 1970s, when the building was razed. The building just visible on the right is the Sisters of St. Joseph Convent at 55 Greig Street, now a New York State Department of Corrections halfway house. Since Greig Street was eliminated, the Correctional facility, which still stands, has driveway access to Ford Street and has adopted a Ford Street address.

Former Sisters of St. Joseph Convent, now a New York State Corrections Department halfway house, that once sat at 55 Greig Street next to Son House's apartment before the latter was razed.

Photo (2014), Janet Mlinar

I'm still digesting the extent of Son House's influence on the world. Even I, an over-the-top fan, am occasionally fooled by his relative obscurity. Son was a key player in fostering modern rock music. He influenced Muddy Waters and Robert Johnson.

Johnson arguably invented rock 'n' roll. He brought blues, the genre of man-woman conflict, from lamentation, a few steps closer to – ironically, celebratory. And he popularized on his acoustic guitar the traveling base beat, the muscle of bop, rockabilly and early rock 'n roll.

Waters spearheaded electric blues, giving AC power, an urban twist and therefore new relevance to music considered rural and becoming passé. Both men re-couched the music of southern agricultural workers, creating the seeds of a previously non-existent musical genre. Waters and Johnson's words and style were soon emulated by white musicians from that city on Lake Michigan, to cities on the Rivers Mersey and Thames.

In his essay, *Self Reliance*, Ralph Waldo Emerson describes how we discover truths in works of art; truths that we already know exist but don't realize we know until we see them expressed by someone else through their art. These truths then emerge from our subconscious to our consciousness. Son House and other blues artists, in fact artists performing and creating in other genres as well, express the feelings many of us know, but deny or are unaware of until they are reflected back at us through their art. In such cases, those artists not only express themselves, they express us for ourselves.

I recently moved to Corn Hill, thirty years, now, after my visit with Son House, in Detroit. I therefore, ironically, became one of those people who I had privately pooh-poohed for driving out most of the former "silent" residents here (including Son) and causing the gentrification of this wonderful old neighborhood. During the move I came across some old CDs. I started listening again to that music that was once so important to me, Son House being apart of that body of work. One day I counted the steps from my apartment in a beautifully-rehabilitated 1853 Italianate mansion, to Son's house, well, the parking lot where it once sat. On the way, I passed through the Lunsford Park traffic circle where, ten years ago, some fellow blues fans and I had placed a makeshift plaque to commemorate Son. A couple people brought guitars and someone brought a bottle of red wine. We had obtained permission from the Neighborhood Association to have this little get-together and place the marker there. It was a bitterly cold March 21st, a Sunday. Guitar strings would have surely snapped and fingernails cracked. So we drove the marker into the frozen ground and huddled in a circle. The Homily was brief; I read aloud the aforementioned vignette about Dick Waterman and Son House walking into the John Hammond club performance in Philadelphia, from *Between Midnight and Day: The Last Unpublished Blues Archive* – then just published. We Then celebrated Communion.

The marker is no longer there. No surprise; it wasn't made of durable material and probably succumbed to the weather. I would like to see in the circle, or somewhere else in the neighborhood, a real memorial to Son House. I envision an interactive scenario: First, his life-size likeness cast in bronze, seated casually in an ice cream parlor-type chair, placed on a small patio, holding his resonator guitar. On the patio, in a circle,

64

would be three or four other empty chairs, facing Son, where musicians or visitors might sit, and join him, impromptu. One of Son's major post-rediscovery legacies is all the people who came to visit him when he lived here. I also envision a couple guitar stands, so one could rest his guitar in order to play the blues harp, or check on the contents of his brown paper bag.

When I did start listening to Son again, I heard him afresh and began contemplating the man, all over again. I recalled a question put to me more than 30 years ago, by Son's wife, Evie: What's in it fer him?! At that time, I had gone on the defensive, taking it as a challenge to my integrity as a fan, even a person. I realize, now, it was Evie, not Son, who was concerned about the value of our visit. Son had an internal imperative to do what he did. He had the music in him and had to give it. He not only sang, he did so joyously, open-handedly. He appeared to have nothing but he gave fully to us. That's what was in it for him.

I wonder what the world would be like if we all did the same thing, sang 'us' for 'us' and in the process, were able to sing 'others' for 'others,' where 'singing' was really whatever skill we could perform better than others.

And there might have been something more in it for him, and for Evie, as well. Based on what I've ascertained from my research, however informal it has been, I imagine our meeting with Son that day was one of the few times he met with fans and there was no smoking and drinking, no bullshitting. We were there to see what Son had to say. I'd been disappointed that he was so "cleaned up," yet that was a unique aspect of our visit. I'd like to ask Evie how she felt about that, but it's too late now.

RSG, 2015
Corn Hill
Rochester, NY

FINDING SON HOUSE: THE FINAL CHAPTER

Searching for Son House: a journey; a goal; hope; anticipation; finally finding Son House. A major life event for me. But, the end of the journey? Actually the beginning, or perhaps, a new beginning. Other life searches aren't necessarily the end of a journey either. Finally finding your life mate is not the end of a journey. Nor finally earning your degree. In a perfect world they are each beginnings; of a marriage, a career. A good life mate can support you in many ways. A good education can propel you forward and upward. For me, tracking down the Father of Folk Blues was the beginning of a spiritual relationship with the blues and a new relationship with life itself. In the beginning the new relationship was personified in this man who was the blues incarnate. From there, I progressed to learn the art of navigation through the other parts of my life. I am now, finally, my own spokesperson. There are, of course other searches – journeys, findings and new beginnings. Likely as many journeys as there are people.

NOTES ON DELTA BLUES

When we see the words "delta" and "Mississippi" in the same sentence we might envision the Mississippi River Delta. That's in Louisiana, somewhere in the vicinity of New Orleans, home of the most famous party in America, the Mardi Gras.

Mississippi Delta vis-à-vis the blues, refers to an area hundreds of miles upriver from New Orleans, in the state of Mississippi. The northwest portion of Mississippi is referred to as the delta land, as in the Yazoo River Delta, also called the Yazoo River Basin. The former flood land is an area the size of Maryland. The terrain is flat, the soil rich. There is no party here, though, at least there wasn't for Negro slaves who hand-worked rice and cotton plantations as big as Northern townships. Predating the plantations were mosquito-infested forests that had to be cleared. By hand. Mostly black hands.

To help the days pass felling trees and harvesting crops, the slaves – and later freed blacks, often sang. Sometimes they sang to each other, one belting out a line and waiting for the next soul a few cotton rows over to repeat it. These were call-and-response hollers.

Example:

(call) O Graveyard
(response) O graveyard
(call) I'm walkin' troo de graveyard
(response) Lay dis body down

NOTES ON GRINNIN' IN YOUR FACE

Don't ya mind people grinnin' in your face,
Don't mind people grinnin' in your face
…yeah…
Just bear this in mind,
A true friend is hard to find.
Don't ya mind people grinnin' in your face.

You know your mother will talk about you,
Your sisters and your brothers, too.
Yes, don't care how you're tryin' to live,
They'll talk about you still…
…yes…
But bear – hooo! – this in mind,
A true friend is hard to find.
Don't ya mind people grinnin' in your face.

Don't mind people grinnin' in your face,
Don't mind people grinnin' in your face…
…ooh…
Just bear – hooo! – this in mind,
A true friend is hard to find.
Don't ya mind people grinnin' in your face,

Ya know they'll jump you up and down,
They'll tear all around 'n' round.

Just as soon as your back a turnin',
They'll be tryin' to crush you down.
Yes but bear this in mind,
A true friend is hard to find.
Don't ya mind people grinnin' in your face.

Don't mind people grinnin' in your face,
Don't mind people grinnin' in your face,
...oh, Lord!...
Just bear – hooo! – this in mind,
A true friend is hard to find.
Don't ya mind people grinnin' in your face.

- SON HOUSE

Son House was known for his twelve-bar blues, signature open-tuned bottleneck guitar, rich baritone voice, and powerful delivery. Ironically, *Grinnin,'* arguably Son's tour de force, although highlighting his powerful baritone, is technically not a blues song and is performed a cappella, without an instrument. He's not alluding to love, sex or booze; he's talking about what he sees as the inherent malice in people.

Grinnin' is a field holler, a precursor of blues. Hollers go back hundreds of years. *Grinnin'* is not call-and-response, but more self-directed. Son is singing to himself and warning anyone within earshot to 'Keep a mind.'

His hand-clapping may seem out of synch with the musical phrases in *'Grinnin,'* but it may not be intended to set the pace. It may be the simulation of the clip-clop of a horse or mule's hooves pulling a load, or the ring of an axe against a tree, or the falling of a sledge against a railroad spike. In another light, the lack of timing in his clapping could be a reflection of the disconnect and isolation the malice of humans makes him feel.

I see *Grinnin'* as Son's personal mantra. Its composition (the world being against you, even your family and friends) and mode of delivery are a true manifestation of the man I met, the man I've studied, and the voice to which I've so often listened. I believe Son was haunted by a super-sized ration of fears, suspicions, sorrows, self-loathing, and regrets. Reverend Carrsellsa Knox, who died on August 23rd, 2013, six days short of her 100th birthday, was interviewed in a 1978 documentary about Son House, on WXXI-TV, in Rochester, New York. In that interview she stated she had met Son in 1937 (when she was 24), and had lived with Son and his wife for a while thereafter. She said he walked around the house singing *Grinnin in your Face'* "…all the time." This is interesting because 1937 is the same year Son turned his back on the Church and started playing the blues. It is therefore likely that *Grinnin,'* similar to another Son House a cappella holler – *John the Revelator,* is a carryover from his gospel singing days.

Whatever the source of *Grinnin,'* its insightful sadness delivered in Son's powerful voice, render it a singular work of cultural art that has not been surpassed in the 77 years since its first appearance, in spite of all the music-enhancing technology that has ensued. This black man sitting in a roadhouse at night, his image illuminated by a single candle, singing *Grinnin,'* will hold the attention of an audience as closely as Pink Floyd, with its 13-member stage show, lasers, train load of amps, and 50-foot display screen.

SON HOUSE: SELECTED DISCOGRAPHY

78 RPM RECORDINGS

Recorded May 28, 1930 in Grafton, WI, for Paramount Records

- Walking Blues (unissued and lost until 1985)
- My Black Mama: Part I
- My Black Mama: Part II
- Preachin' the Blues: Part I
- Preachin' the Blues: Part II
- Dry Spell Blues: Part I
- Dry Spell Blues: Part II
- Clarksdale Moan
- Mississippi County Farm Blues

FIELD RECORDINGS FOR LIBRARY OF CONGRESS/ FISK UNIVERSITY*
RECORDED AUGUST 1941 IN CLACK, MS

- Levee Camp Blues (with Willie Brown, Fiddlin' Joe Martin, Leroy Williams)
- Government Fleet Blues (with Willie Brown, Fiddlin' Joe Martin, Leroy Williams)
- Walking Blues (with Willie Brown, Fiddlin' Joe Martin, Leroy Williams)
- Shetland Pony Blues (with Willie Brown)
- Camp Hollers (with Willie Brown, Fiddlin' Joe Martin, Leroy Williams)
- Delta Blues (with Leroy Williams)
  Recorded July 17, 1942, in Robinsonville, MS
- Special Rider Blues (two takes)
- Low Down Dirty Dog Blues
- Depot Blues
- American Defense

- Am I Right or Wrong?
- Walking Blues
- County Farm Blues
- The Pony Blues
- The Jinx Blues: No. 1
- The Jinx Blues: No. 2
- Several Interviews

* The music from both sessions and most of the recorded interviews have been released on LP and CD

SINGLES

- The Pony Blues/The Jinx Blues: No. 1 (1967)
- Make me a Pallet on the Floor (Willie Brown)/Shetland Pony Blues (1967)
- Death Letter (1985)

OTHER ALBUMS

- The Complete Library of Congress Sessions: Travelin' Man CD 02 (1964)
- Blues from the Mississippi (with J. D. Short), Folkway Records (1964)
- The Legendary Son House: Father of Folk Blues, Columbia Records (1965)
- In Concert (Oberlin College), Stack-o-Hits 9004 (1965)
- Delta Blues (1941 to 1942), Smithsonian 31028
- Son House & Blind Lemon Jefferson (1926 to 1941), Biograph 12040
- Son House: The Real Delta Blues (1964-65 Recordings), Blue Goose Records 2016
- Son House & the Great Delta Blues Singers (with Willie Brown), Document CD 5002
- Son House at Home: Complete 1969, Document 5148
- Son House (Library of Congress), Folk Lyric 9002
- John The Revelator, Liberty 83391
- American Folk Blues Festival '67 (1 cut), Optimism CD 2070

- Son House: 1965 to 1969 (mostly TV appearances), Private Record Pr-01
- Son House: Father of the Delta Blues – Complete 1965, Sony/Legacy CD 48867
- Living Legends (1 cut, 1966), Verve/Folkways 3010
- Real Blues (1 cut, University of Chicago, 1964), Takoma 7081 (1981)
- John The Revelator: 1970 London Sessions, Sequel CD 207

- Great Bluesmen/Newport (2 cuts, 1965), Vanguard CD 77/78
- Blues With a Feeling (3 cuts, 1965) Vanguard CD 77005
- Rare Blues (1 cut), Tacoma Blues Series (Won Grammy, Best Ethnic and Traditional) (1981)
- Son House Bukka White – Masters of the Country Blues, Yazoo Video 500
- Son House: The Legendary 1969 Rochester Sessions Complete, Document Records (Austria) DOCD-5148 (1992)
- Delta Blues and Spirituals (1995)
- In Concert (Live) (1996)
- Live at Gaslight Café, 1965 (2000)
- Son House Revisited, FUEL Records (2002)
- New York Central Live (2003)
- Delta Blues (1941-1942) (2003) Biograph CD 118
- Classic Blues from Smithsonian Folkways, Smithsonian Folkways 40134 (2003)
- Classic Blues from Smithsonian Folkways, Vol. 2, Smithsonian Folkways 40148 (2003)
- Martin Scorsese Presents the Blues: Son House (2003)
- The Very Best of Son House: Heroes of the Blues, Shout! Factory 30251 (2003)
- Proper Introduction to Son House (2004) Proper

Martin Scorsese Presents the Blues: Son House

CONTENT OF EARLY BEATLES ALBUMS

Songs written or first recorded by black Americans are in italics

1: THE BEATLES: PLEASE PLEASE ME," RELEASED MARCH 1963

Track listing:

Ask Me Why: Lennon/McCartney

Do You Want to Know a Secret? Lennon/McCartney

I Saw Her Standing There: Lennon/McCartney

Love Me Do: Lennon/McCartney

Misery: Lennon/McCartney

Please Please Me: Lennon/McCartney

PS I Love You: Lennon/McCartney

There's a Place: Lennon/McCartney

Anna: Arthur Alexander

A Taste of Honey: Bobby Scott, Ric Marlowe (Lenny Welch)

Baby It's You: The Shirelles

Boys: Luther Dixon, Les Farrell (The Shirelles)

Chains: Gerry Goffin, Carole King (The Cookies)

Twist and Shout: Phil Medley, Burt Russell (Isley Brothers)

2: "WITH THE BEATLES," RELEASED NOVEMBER 1963

Track listing:

All I've Got to Do: Lennon/McCartney

All My Loving: Lennon/McCartney

Don't Bother Me: George Harrison

Hold Me Tight: Lennon/McCartney

It Won't Be Long: Lennon/McCartney

I Wanna Be Your Man: Lennon/McCartney

Little Child: Lennon/McCartney

Not a Second Time: Lennon/McCartney

Money: Janie Bradford, Berry Gordy (Barrett Strong)

Please Mr. Postman: Georgia Dobbins, William Garrett, Freddie Gorman, Brian Holland, Robert Bateman (Marvelettes)

Roll Over Beethoven: Chuck Berry

'Til There Was You: Meredith Wilson

You Really Got a Hold on Me: Smokey Robinson (Miracles)

CONTENT OF EARLY ROLLING STONES ALBUMS

The songwriting credit, Nanker Phelge, is contrived, meaning "Composed by all five Rolling Stones" (Mick Jagger, Keith Richards, Brian Jones, Charlie Watts and Bill Wyman). Songs written or first recorded by black Americans in italics:

1: "The Rolling Stones," released April 1964

Track listing:

Now I've Got a Witness: Nanker Phelge

Little by Little: Nanker Phelge and Phil Spector

Tell Me: Jagger and Richards

Can I Get a Witness: Briand Holland, Lamont Dosier, Eddie Holland

Carol: Chuck Berry

Honest I Do: Jimmy Reed

I'm a King Bee: Slim Harpo

I Just Want to Make Love to You: Willie Dixon

Mona: Elias McDaniel aka Bo Diddley

Walking the Dog: Rufus Thomas

You Can Make It If You Try: Ted Jarrett

2: "The Rolling Stones 12 X 5," released October 1964

Track listing:

Congratulations: Jagger/Richards

Empty Heart: Nanker Phelge

Good Times, Bad Times: Jagger/Richards

Grown Up Wrong: Jagger/Richards

2120 South Michigan Avenue: Nanker Phelge

Confessin' the Blues: Jay McShann, Walter Brown

If You Need Me: Wilson Pickett, Robert Bateman

It's All Over Now: Bobby Womack, Shirley Womack

Time Is on My Side: Irma Thomas

Susie Q: Dale Hawkins, Stand Lewis, Eleanor Broadwater

Under the Boardwalk: Arthur Resnick, Kenny Young

You may also want to check out:

Preachin' the Blues:
The Life and Times of Son House
Daniel Beaumont.
(2011, Oxford University Press)
A well-researched life of Son House, the man.

Between Midnight and Day:
The Last Unpublished Blues Archive
Richard Waterman
(2003, Insight Editions)
A memoir, told through original vignettes and
An unparalleled collection of photos,
of managing old blues artists.

Blues Walkin' Like a Man: a Tribute to Son House
Rory Block, 2008, Stony Plain

Please visit and "Like" *10,000 Fans of Son House* Facebook Page

Also:

Last Train to Memphis:
The Rise of Elvis Presley
Peter Guralnick, 1994

Searching for Robert Johnson
Peter Guralnick, 1989

Also by Richard Shade Gardner:

Learning to Walk: Book I of the Trilogy
Amazon, Kindle

Simply New York,
Artizanns

21460672R00058

Made in the USA
Middletown, DE
30 June 2015